The Greedy 1%: Chronicles of a Wall Street Tyrant

Mark D. Mandel, CFA

Copyright © 2012 Mark D. Mandel
All rights reserved.
ISBN-10: 1479294292
EAN-13: 9781479294299
Library of Congress Control Number: 2012917331
CreateSpace Independent Publishing Platform
Noth Charleston, South Carolina

In memory of our friend and colleague,

Brian Gingrich

Acknowledgements

I would like to thank my sister, Laurie, for her guidance and creativity, and my wife, Kimberly, for her support, patience, and assistance.

Preface

In corporate America in general, and on Wall Street in particular, there are no shortages of Type A, extraordinarily driven, and ruthless men and women who have scratched, clawed, and climbed their way to the tops of companies, industries, and governments. In many cases, these individuals use other—lower-ranked and, in their view, less important—colleagues and employees to further their ascension.

On Wall Street, more than anywhere else, the primary motivator is to maximize income. Now, this is not to say that those who toil in other businesses are altruistic, but at least most companies, whether they are producing goods or delivering services, can make a strong case that their output is directly contributing to the greater good of society. The issue of whether or not Wall Street and the greater financial services industry benefits society is currently the subject of fierce debate, thanks to the financial crisis of 2008–2009 and the emergence of the Occupy Wall Street movement. What is difficult to argue, however, is that the vast majority of those who work in the securities industry are highly motivated by the prospect of securing a fat, juicy, year-end bonus, remuneration that often dwarfs their annual six-figure salaries.

This book is designed to recount, in an entertaining and humorous way, how one senior Wall Street analyst, Merv Moneymax, already the recipient of millions of dollars in compensation from a fifteen-year career at a leading firm, rebuilt his lucrative "franchise" while running roughshod over subordinates and other colleagues. It is hard to quarrel with a person getting a second chance to further, or rebuild, a career, even doing so in an ultra-competitive manner. But the manner in which Merv pursued his Wall Street career—abusive towards his associates and, at times, unethically—was repugnant. There are plenty of highly competitive and motivated people on The Street, but the vast majority approach their jobs with a high degree of conscientiousness and integrity. This book is not meant to imply that Merv Moneymax is the norm, for he certainly is not. In this writing, most names are fictitious to protect the innocent and abused.

Introduction

The year 1992 marked the tenth anniversary of what was to become known as the Great Bull Market, a meteoric rise in equity prices that eventually spanned a twenty-year period. As with any bull market, this one had its down periods, and 1992, which represented the midpoint of stocks' great run, was highlighted by an economic recession. During recessions, or more accurately the months leading up to an economic downturn, stock prices typically decline substantially, as the market discounts, or prices, an expected fall in corporate earnings. These are also periods when employment and compensation fall on Wall Street, as securities firms try to stem the flow of red ink by chopping compensation expense, which can run to 50 percent or more of company revenue.

Merv Moneymax's departure from Bullhorn Securities in 1991 was not your typical Wall Street head-chopping. For Merv had built a profitable mini-empire by assembling a team of analysts, assistants, and secretaries (what administrative assistants were called in the old days) covering the retail industry. Bullhorn was one of the largest firms in the securities industry, with a highly acclaimed retail and institutional brokerage business, an enormous money-management operation, and a successful investment banking presence. The consumer and retail banking group at Bullhorn thrived by participating in the initial public offerings (IPOs) of many of the specialty retailers that burst onto the American retail scene during the rapid economic expansion of the 1980s, a period that saw the likes of Staples and TJX go public. Instead of showing gratitude for Merv's fifteen-year role in supporting the efforts of Bullhorn's research and banking efforts, the senior folks, many of whom had long since tired of Merv's abusive, morale-busting style, ousted him. The possible reasons for Merv's exit are many, and one can only speculate based on circumstantial evidence, but one thing is clear: Merv was as difficult a person to work with as they come. His forced exit ignited a celebration, with former associates dancing in the halls.

After Merv's abrupt departure from Bullhorn Securities, it was only a matter of weeks before he "landed" at TradeHouse Securities, a large, trading-oriented firm that was attempting to strengthen its stock research and investment banking departments. Since TradeHouse had a gaping hole in the research coverage of the important Retail Industry, thanks to the untimely departure of a senior analyst responsible for that sector, it did not take an experienced matchmaker to put two and two together. So despite understandable concerns about adding the controversial Moneymax to their staff, TradeHouse's Director of Research and head of consumer investment banking hired him at the end of 1991.

Merv stood just over six feet tall and weighed about two hundred pounds. Other than a small midsection paunch, he was not the worst physical specimen. He was bald across most of the top of his head, which he tried to hide with a feeble "comb-over." His hair color had sort of an orange tint to it, most likely the result of some over-the-counter coloring product. Merv's hands were as soft as any man's, which was not surprising since it was highly unlikely he ever changed a light bulb, let alone a tire—plus the fact that for some strange reason he hated to wash his hands, even after using the restroom. You learn a lot about someone when you travel with him, and as Merv's right-hand man, this was unavoidable.

To say that his coworkers viewed Merv's lack of basic hygiene with disgust would be an understatement. Unfortunately, there was not much that could be done about it, other than taking basic precautions such as trying to shake the hands of unsuspecting clients *before* Merv had the opportunity to spread his wealth of germs. And for some strange and inexplicable reason, Merv hated to use urinals. But he also couldn't be bothered to lift a toilet seat first. At TradeHouse's offices, this annoying habit persisted until someone posted a note on the bathroom door requesting that the inconsiderate culprit "at least have the decency to lift the seat."

Merv dressed like a Wall Streeter—polished wing-tip shoes, expensive suits, and white—always white—button-down shirts. When he entered his office, the suit jacket came off, and he rolled up his sleeves, as if to pretend he was ready to get his germ-infested hands dirty. During the summer, Merv wore short-sleeved button-down shirts like some shoe salesman from the 1950s.

Merv's office was fairly spartan. Except for a couple of books and a few framed pictures of his three children, the office was empty. It always looked like he was ready for a hasty retreat, as if he were a traveling salesman ready to pull up his stakes and move on. His briefcase never had a scratch on it, probably because he barely kept anything in it—a couple of notepads, pens, a few other odds and ends, and a box of Gas-X. It was unclear what was in Merv's diet that would cause that much indigestion. More than likely his demeanor, which resembled an active volcano on the cusp of an eruption, was a leading cause of gastric distress. Merv had his daily ritual—he came into the office at 8:00 a.m., out came the pads and pens, and dashing off to the cafeteria went one of the two secretaries to fetch cans of Diet Pepsi and a supersized cup of coffee, black, no sugar. On most days, the soda did not get opened, and the coffee was barely sipped, for the level of intensity and the pace Merv kept didn't allow time for any indulgence.

All day long, or so it seemed, Merv scratched out memos while others typed and proofread them and wrote research reports. His work was all about speed and volume, as opposed to deep proprietary research. There were some exceptions, but for the most part, Merv's office resembled a command-and-control center for some crucial, time-sensitive operation, with people scurrying in and out throughout the day. Merv was big with hand gestures. Rotating his right hand in an outward, circular motion meant speed up your gait or speech. Merv usually kept his door shut, so motioning others to enter his lair, even as they were about to—but not at an acceptable speed—was another. Upon entering Merv's office, he would often blurt out "Go" as a request to say quickly what was on your mind.

On one occasion, Merv's abruptness was especially annoying and inconsiderate. Bill, who was Merv's first hire and always in the office before the 8:00 *Express* rolled onto the thirty-sixth floor, was on the phone with his insurance company trying to resolve an issue. The process was taking longer than he expected, and by 8:00, he was still working on the problem when Merv came flying around the corner, jacket and briefcase in hand with the free arm summoning the troops into the command center. Bill held up his index finger in a desperate attempt to plead for one minute to wrap up his call, a gesture that Merv considered insubordinate. As he barreled past Bill's office with an angry look on his face, he tapped on the glass wall and pointed in the direction of his office. Bill was not about to let fifteen minutes of problem resolution go down the drain, so he ignored Merv's request and the subsequent banging on the wall that separated their two offices. After his call, he entered Merv's office where the team had gathered for its daily briefing. Merv was so furious, we all would later agree that we could see smoke wafting from his ears as Merv's face turned red and the veins on his neck pulsated.

To be sure, there was some rationale for being expedient, especially when the group was publishing its analysis of a company's financial results, for Merv knew all too well that clients were getting bombarded with research, and if your report was the fifteenth, tenth, or even fifth on their desk, chances were it would be ignored. In those days, research was distributed by "snail mail" (aka The US Postal Service), and getting reports submitted to TradeHouse's editorial staff and then off to the publisher was critical. Entering reports into the queue was important because it was first come/first served, except for time-sensitive events such as a major acquisition or merger announcement. So to try to game, or "abuse", the system, Merv would submit reports, even if they were still in rough shape. Mary, the chief editor, had seen all the tricks, however, and she usually stood up to Merv's insincere attempts to sweet-talk his reports to the top of the list.

Merv probably kept the most predictable schedule of anyone on Wall Street, an industry where long hours and six- and even seven-day weeks are not unusual. But not Moneymax. As predictable as his arrival was each morning at 8:00 sharp, when 5:00 p.m. rolled around, it was best not to be physically positioned between Merv's office door and the elevator bank. It was almost like he would turn into a pumpkin or was escaping from an erupting volcano. With one move of his arm, everything on his desk—pens, pads, unopened cans of Diet Pepsi—was swept into the trash. Nearly full cups of coffee—ice cold by now—were placed on the credenza by the secretary's desk for maintenance to dispose of when they made their rounds later that evening. He would grab his jacket and briefcase and run for the elevators. Anyone who got in his way risked collision. One day it was Marge, an analyst of formidable size, who was heading to her office with a cup of coffee, one she intended to drink, when Merv rounded the corner, sending the coffee and Marge flying. Merv managed to squeeze out a quick apology before disappearing into the closing elevator, leaving a stunned and furious Marge drenched with coffee and the thought of a large dry cleaning bill. For lunch, Merv ate a plastic container of cantaloupe that one of his secretaries brought back from the cafeteria. To our surprise, a brief lunch break was permitted, but Merv wouldn't take the time other than pauses for a few bites of his fruit.

In his mid-forties, with two kids entering the college pipeline, and a large house in one of the New York area's most expensive suburbs, Moneymax was not thinking of retirement. Just as important, Merv's goal of placing first in the annual *Institutional Investor (II)* magazine's survey of analysts repeatedly fell short by one with his rival analyst at Wall Street's most prestigious firm maintaining his long-running first-place finish. This survey, which produces these highly valued rankings, easily translates into lucrative pay packages for the analysts who land in the top slots, fueling an all-out effort to capture as many votes as possible from institutional investors when they cast their ballots each May. Although consistently ranking second in an industry with scores of analysts is certainly nothing to be ashamed of, for ultra-competitive Merv Moneymax, this ranking was simply not acceptable. There is nothing wrong with the competitive spirit bringing out the best products and services from individuals or companies, but a "win-at-all-costs" mentality often emerges from intensely competitive conditions, and Merv fell right into this trap.

In addition to formulating stock recommendations, analysts are also supposed to apply financial analysis (imagine that) to generate financial forecasts, with sales and earnings estimates the highlights of these efforts. In fact, over the long run, a company's stock price should correlate with its earnings per share (EPS) performance, although numerous other factors certainly come into play. EPS are so important, that analysts' ability to produce accurate estimates is measured by a number of high-profile organizations including *The Wall Street Journal*. Moneymax understood this all too well, but his method of estimating earnings of the companies he followed was anything but the result of thoughtful financial analysis. Basically, Merv would get a company's investor relations contact on the phone, and, after a few macho-esque give-and-takes, would ask the now-beleaguered executive what the current consensus estimate was, even though analysts' earnings estimates were aggregated by numerous organizations and made public. Merv would then propose setting his estimate well above the consensus, knowing full well that the response would be something on the order of, "Well, Merv, I can't tell you what to set your estimate at, but that figure is a bit aggressive." Merv would usually counter with something between the consensus estimate and his blatantly high figure. Company executives rarely liked seeing analysts publishing inflated estimates, since this created a higher hurdle for the company to clear when it reported its financial results. When a company announces earnings that exceed consensus forecasts, that firm's stock price usually increases, a favorable reflection on the senior executives. There was a method to Merv's madness, however. With the economy coming out of recession by late 1992, most retailers were starting to show stronger financial results. Normally, this resulted in earnings that exceeded analysts' forecasts. Merv's strategy tended to produce EPS forecasts that were more accurate than his peers', a coup de grâce that Merv flaunted like his head of orange, comb-over hair. The rest of the financial modeling was easy and involved working backwards to make the income statement, as well as balance sheet and cash flow projections "fit" the EPS starting point.

Another example of Merv's abuse of power came when he was the head of a committee that polled investors on topics such as the best corporate investor relations officials and the most effective annual reports. It's still a mystery how Merv pulled that one off—a position typically reserved for the more esteemed members of the financial industry. Moneymax was supposed to query a diverse and statistically meaningful number of institutional investors for their opinions. Did Merv allocate the time necessary to fulfill his duties as chairperson? Yeah, right. He would call a few of his closest buy-side counterparts or fax them a survey form (to which most didn't respond) to cover his ass. Then *he* would pick the winners that would generate some goodwill from these companies. Merv shrewdly knew that there would be no way to prove an abuse of power, and most people were too busy to even care. Merv didn't even bother to hide his methods from his subordinates since he calculated (correctly) that they also figured the injustice was trivial enough to let slide. "Why would Merv even bother since the results of the poll had little, if any, importance", they wondered.

Marriage of Inconvenience

Merv tried to lure Bill to Bullhorn's retail team in 1989 after one of its analysts suddenly left for more sedate pastures. But Bill was happy covering retail and other industries for Shield Insurance Company, and he also had heard of Merv's reputation as a "difficult" person to work with. As a client of Merv and Bullhorn's retail group, Bill never saw Merv's (or any other analyst's) dark side, but he knew it existed in some form. In Bill, Merv saw a reasonably bright young analyst and, more importantly, someone of the same gender that he could effectively control. There could be only one cook in

Merv's kitchen, and other than his secretaries, this kitchen was too hot for any woman, lest they complain about Merv's foul mouth and overbearing personality.

Nineteen ninety-one brought about a different set of circumstances. With a recession taking its toll, as they usually do, on the US economy in general, and weaker-performing companies, in particular, the Shield Insurance Company was struggling to keep its head above water. The company had notoriously high expense-and-loss ratios, and the recession was exacerbating both. Employees at Shield were growing nervous, and Bill, who had just purchased his first house, was expecting a second child, fueling his concerns that his ten-year career might hit a speed bump.

By late 1991, with the economy deteriorating, Merv was out at Bullhorn. Professionals who have achieved success during a fifteen-year tenure at a leading company rarely leave empty-handed, and Merv's departure was no exception. However, along with a handsome severance package came a stipulation that Merv was not to bring any of his former associates to whatever new firm he joined. Not that any of his former co-workers were anxious to sustain a tortuous working relationship with Merv, but Bullhorn didn't want to risk losing any up-and-coming stars in the retail group and didn't want to see the team gutted, given its importance to the investment bankers. Besides, the top dogs at Bullhorn already had their sights set on Merv's replacement, and they wanted the new senior retail analyst to join a fully assembled team to avoid any unnecessary disruption in front of the approaching *Institutional Investor* voting season.

The Shield ship was starting to take on water, and with Moneymax set to join his new firm, TradeHouse Securities, Merv, once again, reached out to his client Bill in an attempt to help him build his next empire. Bill was leery of joining the "Sell-Side," as the broker-dealer side of Wall Street is known, and leaving the "Buy-Side," but the appeal of maintaining consistent employment and the lure of a 60 percent hike in pay was simply too much to resist. The interviews with the Director of Research and Deputy Director of Research were basically formalities. Senior analysts can usually hire whom they want as assistants and often bring one along with them when they change firms, but as explained earlier, this was not possible for Merv. So Merv lured Bill into his den with the understanding that Bill would, sooner rather than later, cover as a licensed analyst his own companies as opposed to solely assisting Merv with his agenda. Bill joined TradeHouse Securities as a junior analyst and Merv's subordinate.

The working relationship between the two got off to an amicable enough start. Bill was an easy-going guy who got along with just about anyone and found some humor in Merv's "rough edges" and "bad table manners," or whatever you wanted to call his daily habits. This was important because the initial physical arrangement was anything but ideal, with Merv and Bill subject to sharing Merv's office.

Bill sat across from Merv's desk with a stack of boxes serving as his makeshift desk. Day One served to shed some light on how Merv approached his job as a senior analyst. He handed Bill a list of companies that would mark the foundation of the retail group's coverage, including companies such as Toys R Us, Home Depot, Woolworth, Melville, Wal-Mart, Kmart, Dayton Hudson, J. C. Penney, May Department Stores, and Federated Department Stores. All total, about a dozen names made up the initial list—certainly a reasonable starting point given that the average coverage list for most analysts is about fifteen companies. Merv's list allowed for some future expansion, an important selling point to potential investment-banking clients.

Merv then asked Bill to note what his investment recommendations would be. Back in the early 1990s—before scandals such as Worldcom and Enron rocked the securities business, precipitating tighter controls such as Regulation FD (Fair Disclosure) and Eliot Spitzer's crusade—most investment banks, including TradeHouse, used a five-point system to assign investment ratings to stocks. A typical structure would use labels such as Strong Buy, Buy, Hold or Neutral, Sell, and Strong Sell, with the last two rarely used. The basic premise was that analysts could appease bankers and the companies they were targeting with a preponderance of Strong Buy and Buy ratings, even if they were only lukewarm at best about the stock's prospects. A Hold rating would be used for companies and their stocks that the analysts had a genuine negative sentiment towards.

Bill, who spent the last five years picking stocks for Shield Insurance Company, jotted down a list of ratings that closely resembled a bell-shaped curve, albeit with somewhat more Buys than Sells. After handing the list back to Merv, the senior of the two exhibited a smirk while proceeding to alter the list of ratings to reflect a large number of Strong Buys and Buys with a sprinkling of Holds. In the world according to Merv, clients really didn't care about an analyst's ratings. In reality, Merv's goals were basically two-fold: maximize his contribution to and support of the investment bankers and move to the top of the II rankings in the retail category.

Investment banking and research are designed to serve two distinct, but often conflicting, clients. Wall Street bankers help corporate clients raise capital that these companies use to fund their growth and offer these clients strategic advice in areas such as mergers & acquisitions and divestitures of unwanted businesses. Research's primary function is to provide sound advice and knowledge of industries and companies to institutional money managers and individuals. Before the scandals that rocked Wall Street at the turn of the 21st Century, investment banking departments (aka Corporate Finance) typically financed half of the operating budget of a firm's research department. In addition, research analysts at many large Wall Street firms received compensation for investment banking underwritings within their research coverage universe. These cost allocation and compensation structures represented obvious conflicts of interest that the participants and industry regulators overlooked until the dot com implosion shed light on several instances of abuse.

The maniacal pursuit of these goals was nonstop, albeit with a few rare exceptions. The first came just after Merv and Bill set up shop. The IRS was auditing Merv's taxes, and this issue had to be dealt with immediately. Merv brought in a folder about three inches thick with prior tax returns, supporting documents, and other odds-and-ends. Bill's assignment—make three copies *of everything*! By now, Bill knew better than to question Merv's sense of priorities. So for an entire morning, Bill stood in the mailroom photocopying Merv Moneymax's recent financial history, including key financial details of his departure from Bullhorn Securities.

Therefore, it was no surprise that business as usual came to a screeching halt once again when Merv's daughter attempted to gain entrance into a prominent Midwestern university. Apparently, Jane Moneymax's grades made her acceptance a stretch even for a master yoga instructor, making the required writing sample even more important. The margin of error was basically zero. Merv reassigned several members of his team from report-writing and memo editing to "rewriting" Jane's essay. Finally, Merv used his influence with the CFO of a major Michigan-based company, plus a handsome donation to the school, to lock up his daughter's acceptance. Now, it was back to work.

Analysts then, and now, have several ways to impress their clients and maximize their votes. Good stock picking still holds sway with many institutional investors, and many analysts are recognized for their financial models and the accuracy of their sales and earnings estimates. More importantly, analysts are expected to become a critical source of knowledge of the companies and industries they cover. Finally, through their strong relations with company managements, analysts provide clients, especially important ones, with opportunities to interface with company officials, such as CEOs and CFOs (aka corporate access). This role has become increasingly important in recent years, but was also a service in demand twenty years ago. It is this function that Moneymax built his franchise on, and his ultra-aggressive, never-take-no-for-an-answer attitude produced its intended results.

Assembling the Team

The term *team* was as strong a misnomer as one could find when describing the structure of TradeHouse's retail industry research staff. A bona fide team implies a group of people working toward a common goal and greater good. The team Merv put together had one overriding objective: to maximize Merv's image and income. Any other benefits or crumbs that happened to fall through the cracks were merely incidental. Be that as it were, from research department and investment banking standpoints, having a competitive retail research effort that covered the primary bases—General Merchandise, Hardlines, Softlines, and Food and

Drugstore—was important. So, after the initial triumvirate of Merv, Bill, and secretary Sharon, the Director of Research gave Merv the green light to expand. Merv essentially had four characteristics that he looked for in assessing candidates for the position of analyst or assistant: first, they had to be male; second, he considered only Type B personalities who could be controlled; third, he looked for someone who was intelligent; and finally, he wanted someone who was able to write and edit.

Richard was the first victim recruited. A slight, bespectacled lad from the Midwest, Richard made a perfect assistant for Merv. He was soft-spoken, very smart, and had an excellent ability to write, and he wasn't likely to make any demands to move up to analyst. Next on the agenda was a softlines analyst. Softlines is just another way of saying apparel and footwear retailing. Companies back in the 1990s that fell into this category included Gap Stores, The Limited, Ann Taylor, and The TJX Companies. A majority of the analysts covering this space are women, but plenty of male analysts have done a credible job following these firms also. Merv turned to Bill to provide him with the names of candidates for this position, but Bill was reluctant to lure anyone he knew, and certainly anyone he admired, into the cauldron. Finally, under relentless pressure to provide at least one name, Bill mentioned a friend and former colleague from his days at Shield as a possibility, thinking that his friend would have little, if any, interest in joining TradeHouse.

Ben was actually a fixed-income analyst at Shield, but he worked with the small equity team on a couple of projects. Ben proved himself to be an excellent, diligent analyst with a soft demeanor and was a pleasure to work with. Bill and Ben hit it off right away and quickly became good friends. After Bill departed Shield for TradeHouse, Ben decided to stick around for a while longer. Ben was part of a solid, fixed-income team at Shield that was responsible for managing close to $10 billion (most of the financial assets of property and casualty insurance companies are invested in fixed-income securities as opposed to equities).

Bill didn't expect the phone call to Ben inviting him to come over and meet Merv to go anywhere. To Bill's surprise, however, Ben was not only receptive to the idea but greeted the overture enthusiastically. Trying to nip this development in the bud—the last thing Bill wanted to do was lure Ben into an extremely unpleasant situation—Bill tried to lay out without mincing words what environment Ben was considering joining if given the chance. "Ben", Bill warned, "we are talking about a first-class whack-job and a den of back-stabbing sharks. Plus, do you really want to cover the apparel retail area?" But for whatever reason—perhaps Ben saw the ongoing deterioration at Shield and was looking to escape—Ben appeared nonplussed by Bill's warnings and, after meeting Merv, soon found himself going through the ritual of interviewing with key people in other departments, including sales, trading, and banking. Ben joined Moneymax's retail team shortly thereafter.

After Ben officially joined the TradeHouse retail team, he was followed by George, who moved from the West Coast to cover the supermarkets and drugstores. John was hired from the same firm that employed Richard—"Back to the well," chortled Merv. John represented another good fit, much like Richard. John grew up in a military family, so discipline and following commands seemed to run in his blood. Peter would eventually join to assist both Bill and George. Expecting Wall Street analysts to share anything is asking a lot. In most instances, however, Bill and George were both easygoing guys who were quite capable of apportioning Peter's time in a civil manner, so this arrangement did not prove to be a problem. Of course, their styles and personalities were perfect for Merv, who now had all the pieces to his team that he could effectively control.

Field Trips, Conferences, Road Shows, and Conference Calls

The Merv Moneymax vote-maximizing model was built upon providing interfaces between clients and companies; not just the dozen or so retailers that Merv officially covered, but other retailers that were expected to go public and retailers covered by other members of his team of analysts. There are many ways to accomplish this, and Wall Street has become more creative in the types of events that will further this goal.

One example is a relatively new conference format in which participating corporate managements agree to spend a full day or a half day in a room (usually at a hotel) meeting with institutional investors either one-on-one or in small groups. This differs from the traditional conference structure where managements give a canned, preplanned presentation in front of a large audience. These corporate officials also may agree to meet with investors in separate one-on-one meetings or in small "break-out sessions" held in a separate room immediately following their presentation and brief question-and-answer period. Analysts will also try to set up conference calls with industry experts or consultants or arrange field trips to visit company headquarters or divisions. Unlike basic research, providing corporate access to clients normally results in a more immediate and direct payback as money managers may direct extra trades through the sponsoring broker's trading desk. Analysts may also receive important research votes from their buy-side clients that figure into the allocation of trading commissions.

During Merv's rise to recognition, he relied on three primary vehicles to capture the attention of investors: Field trips, seminars, and conference calls. His annual Retail Field Trip featured a three-day visit to an attractive Sunbelt city, such as Las Vegas, Phoenix, Dallas, or Atlanta. This event required many months of planning and had to be choreographed perfectly to avoid any disruptive scheduling or traveling disasters. The timing of this event was also important, so as not to conflict with events from competing Wall Street firms, holidays, or periods when many retailers report their quarterly results. Vote maximization was always the overriding goal. In addition to the II voting that took place in May, Greenwich Research Associates held its own survey in February and, while not considered as important as the II vote, these results were factored into analysts' standing within their firms and, hence, compensation.

At Bullhorn Securities, Merv held his Field Trip in late January, just in front of the Greenwich Voting and well before most retailers reported their year-end financial results (fiscal years for a vast majority of retailers end on or about January 31). After he moved to TradeHouse, Merv zeroed in on the week immediately following Thanksgiving because of the peaking interest and importance of retail results in the holiday season and the relative proximity to the voting season. The problem with this date was that since the Field Trip commenced early Monday morning, attendees, personnel at the host venue, clients, and the management of the retail company scheduled first had to cut short their Thanksgiving weekend in order to travel and prepare for the big event. But Merv couldn't care less about any inconveniences that befell others.

Final preparations for the annual Field Trip had to be made on site with a meeting of key hotel conference personnel. Now, these poor folks had at this point probably had enough of Merv, thanks to countless phone calls and faxes (this was before e-mail, remember) and badgering, all with an often condescending tone. Merv delegated very little when it came to key events, for he had the time to take command since he generally couldn't be bothered with performing thorough proprietary research and financial analysis. Those functions, which Merv considered distractions but other analysts and clients considered extremely important, were left to his assistants and junior analysts. Merv's persistence, the tone of his voice, and the importance of the event for the host venue demanded that he receive VIP treatment—or at least quick responses and answers. So if it meant stepping away from family for a few hours on the Sunday after Thanksgiving to meet with a bunch of New York Wall Streeters, so be it. For Bill and the other members of the Retail team, not only was the Sunday traveling unpleasant, but the upcoming meeting with the hotel associates was especially awkward because of guilt by association.

Timing was everything with these events. Investors got to mix with the managements of about eleven companies over a three-day period. On Monday morning, Retailer A would host a breakfast at the base hotel, with management giving a presentation followed by a question-and-answer period. At roughly 10:00 a.m., several buses would transport the group to one of the retailer's stores. Management officials would travel on the buses and answer additional questions. At the store, the investors would break into small groups for tours conducted by either a senior executive, regional manager, or store management. Of course, these stores were presented in the best possible light. In reality, how often did one expect to walk into a Kmart and see clean, well-stocked shelves with a team of smiling, enthusiastic store personnel directing traffic to *Blue-Light Specials?*

Immediately following the tour of Retailer A's store, it was back on the buses, where the management of Retailer B was waiting to travel with us to their showcase store. After the tour, the group would typically convene in the store's back room for an executive *Happy Meal* and a management presentation. In the afternoon, it was yet another company, with the day ending at a restaurant for the final management presentation. By the end of the day, investors had the chance to meet with the managements of four companies. The same exercise was repeated Day Two and Day Three, although the final day ended by late afternoon. That gave everyone a chance to catch an early evening flight home, which was for the majority, back to the Northeast or Midwest. If the Field Trip's location was in the West, it was the red-eye back to New York for Merv's team, for the next day was the first Thursday of the month and that meant the major retailers would be reporting their monthly sales results. No rest for the weary.

Merv, with his own brand of flair, arranged for TradeHouse to pay for the services of a noted retail industry consultant to attend these Field Trips to speak with clients. Many at TradeHouse thought it was odd for a senior industry analyst to hire a consultant for clients since the analysts were paid for their knowledge and expertise, but Merv didn't care what the sales force or others thought. Whatever it took to gain client votes. In fact, as Merv stated on many occasions,

"There are only four important people here: Collin Johnson, Don Kemp, Christine Sawtelle, and John Burns. Nobody else matters." These four represented TradeHouse's CEO, and the heads of research, banking, and sales. We had no doubt that Merv really believed that—he reminded us more than a few times how "we were all commodities and were replaceable."

These trips were Moneymax at his best. I am sure that somewhere over the years there was a snafu—a management team that got delayed or a bus that got lost—but these sojourns were about as flawless as you could expect, and heaven help a retail team member or host city official who screwed up.

Each spring (just in front of the II vote), the TradeHouse retail team sponsored an all-day retail conference, preceded by a dinner for retail company executives of both private and publicly traded companies. The conference in general—and the dinner in particular—was a big deal for the Consumer Investment Banking Group because this gave them an opportunity to highlight their services and resources. Getting a strong speaker to address the dinner crowd was crucial, and Merv set out to secure the top dog of TradeHouse. CEOs, especially of large Wall Street firms, are a tough lot to get any time from, and this situation was made even more difficult by the fact that TradeHouse was in the midst of a major scandal surrounding allegations that the firm tried to corner, of all things, the US Government Bond Market. But remember, Merv didn't take no for an answer, so when CEO Collin Johnson balked, Merv simply turned up the pressure by sending numerous faxes and phone calls to his office. Finally, Johnson called Merv's immediate superior, Director of Research Kemp, asking him "to get Moneymax off of my back." The rest of the retail team was astonished at how aggressive Merv could be when his interests were at stake.

Conference calls were yet another method of maximizing visibility with clients. Companies conducted quarterly conference calls in conjunction with their financial results twenty years ago, just as they do now. However, in the pre-Regulation FD era, companies were more willing to accommodate analysts' requests for their own calls with investors and were somewhat more loose-lipped than they are today. In 2000, the SEC adopted Regulation FD which changed how companies communicated with investors. Reg FD mandated that all publicly held companies disclose information that should be considered material (or likely to move a stock's price) to all investors—large institutions to individuals—at the same time. But in the earlier period, mid-quarter updates were considered useful, and Merv pushed his company contacts, in his aggressive style, to allow TradeHouse to host these events. Merv would usually badger the company official, typically the head of investor relations, until he or she cried uncle. It was less painful in the long run to just do the event than to say no. Besides, Merv was just as aggressive getting clients to sign up for his events, whether they were field trips or conference calls. Merv encouraged Bill and the other junior analysts to host conference calls for their companies, but only so Merv could use that platform for his own advantage. Merv, the irrefutable captain of the ship, made the initial introduction before handing the call over to his deckhand.

Merv, the Memo King

Merv's primary method of communication was the old-fashioned memo. These memos, carefully prepared with assistance from the team, served multiple purposes—outlining his plans, boasting of his accomplishments, and, most importantly, making demands of some sort or another. E-mail hadn't taken root as a broad medium of communication, but memos could still be typed (on a computer), printed, and faxed. Merv started this process by scratching out a draft on a legal-size yellow pad, after which he would dictate (since no one could possibly read his chicken-scratch) the contents to either one of his two administrative assistants—yes, even Merv succumbed to the more progressive term for secretary—or a junior analyst. Initial copies were then distributed to the juniors for editing until a final version was ready. Merv didn't just put out an occasional memo, but rather a steady flow, with activity spiking around marketing events such as conference calls and field trips. Memos were regularly sent to the Director of Research, the institutional sales department, the head of the consumer banking group, company managements, and probably his own wife. They were hand delivered, and they went via fax. On occasion, Merv would bring some work to Bill's house to complete by the next day—not an unreasonable request. Now, a normal, decent person would have at least walked the ten feet from the driveway to the front door, but Merv preferred leaning on the horn of his new Cadillac—a horn that sounded more like a foghorn on an ocean liner on an otherwise quiet residential street. Unfortunately, Bill's six-month-old baby was breast-feeding, with the ear-splitting noise giving him a long-term fear of large cars (and big ships).

Bill lived just ten minutes away in a neighboring town—and at times Bill had to drop off a report at Merv's house. The first time Bill met the lion in his lair, he was summoned to the basement, where he found Merv pedaling furiously on a stationary bicycle, huffing and puffing while he scratched away on his yellow pad. Above, hanging from the ceiling, was a TV tuned to reruns of *F-Troop*, and scattered on the floor, a sampling of memos and other notes written on the familiar legal-size yellow notepad paper. Among the memos was usually tomorrow's agenda under the impersonal, condescending title: "Things for *Them* to Do." How heart-warming, the team thought, to be a part of *them*. "*Well, tomorrow promises to be another intellectually stimulating day*", thought Bill.

So there it was—memo ground zero. Most of the memos, like everything else, were centered on planned and upcoming marketing events. Once the details were ironed out between participating managements and TradeHouse personnel, the next step was to communicate with the sales force and clients.

With a marketing event such as a TradeHouse-sponsored conference call set, the next step was to maximize client participation and recognition of Moneymax's role and visibility. Since competition was fierce and with all the conferences and field trips that retail analysts were sponsoring, it was easy for clients to forget who delivered what. Merv's philosophy was that no one was going to out-muscle him. The first fax to clients was sent well in advance of scheduled events. For major events like the Field Trip, it could be more than six months ahead of time. Even for a mid-quarter conference call, faxes started surfacing at clients' offices months ahead of time and increased in frequency leading up to the event. In fact, it was not unusual for clients to receive half a dozen notices and reminders of a conference call.

No Friend of the Environment

Memos were just the tip of the iceberg when it came to paper flow. The general sentiment among Wall Street analysts is "publish or perish." It is considered important when trying to maximize your visibility and convince clients that you are the "go-to" authority on the stocks and industry you cover. Once again, Merv was going to out-blast his competition. At its peak, Merv's team consisted of nine people: four senior analysts including Merv, Bill (who now covered about a dozen of his own names), Ben, a softlines analyst, and George, who followed the supermarket/drugstore group. Directly reporting and assisting Merv were two administrative assistants and two junior associates. George and Bill shared a junior, rounding out the team. Today, staffing of equity teams is more skewed toward the research side, as admins may report to multiple analysts, thanks to the automation of functions such as expense reports and travel bookings.

Merv really played the role of a company cheerleader, as opposed to someone who objectively analyzed companies' business prospects, management team, and financial statements. The investment bankers were always targeting the companies the research analysts followed and, in many cases, were *suggesting* which companies should be covered with the aim of securing future assignments for stock and debt underwritings, or mergers and acquisitions (M&A) advice. Fifty years old, today, and the largest retailer in the world, Wal-Mart was already the most powerful retailer back in the early 1990s when founder Sam Walton passed away. At that time, Merv got the brilliant idea of publishing a report on the company that would truly stand out from the multitude of research reports constantly hitting clients' desks. Merv's plan was to harness all the troops and produce a one hundred-page tome that he called *The Wal-Mart Encyclopedia.* So forget the fact that Bill, George, and Ben had their own companies to follow; it was all hands on deck for Merv's latest, and most grandiose, research project. This product, which would have all the information on the most important retailer in the world, was going to make Merv look great in the eyes of the bankers and Wal-Mart management, and the clients should appreciate having all this information on the most important retailer in the world. Reports of this magnitude have more "shelf life" than the typically thin research report, increasing Merv's visibility and client votes.

Like everything else Merv produced, *The Encyclopedia* was put together urgently and quickly. Pieces were doled out to the staff and requests went out to Wal-Mart's investor relations people for assistance with lists, maps, and other information. TradeHouse's editors and publishers were engaged, while the Director of Research and head of consumer investment banking were apprised of Merv's monumental effort.

When the work was done, it was time to bombard the investment community with this one hundred-page collection of lists, maps, economic summaries, and descriptions of Wal-Mart's growing retail empire. The absence of any truly trend-setting, unique evaluation of the company's business prospects didn't really matter to Merv, for it was quantity that took center stage. Besides, how many clients, thought Merv, would actually take the time to read the report cover-to-cover?

Whether they read the report or not, Merv was going to make sure they, and just about everyone else, would receive at least two copies. Remember, this was the pre-e-mail period, so research reports were ordered and mailed. Each analyst had his or her own mailing list the publisher used to distribute the research. Merv, however, didn't fully trust anyone to accomplish his or her task, so redundancies were built into everything, from booking flights to publishing research. Merv decided that, in addition to the automated distribution of the Wal-Mart report, he would order additional copies sent to his office for a mailing to clients, managements, media, and anyone else he considered important. Well, Merv's mailing list of clients and management officials from countless retailers, public and private, totaled about 1,300. Of course, thought Merv, better to order more than that just in case we run out. The problem with this strategy is that when you order 1,500 copies of a 100-plus page report, you are talking about a lot of paper.

The delivery came early on a cold, winter day. One by one, the movers wheeled in boxes of reports to Merv's office on the thirty-sixth floor. Quickly, it became apparent that until the reports were mailed, a serious storage problem was at hand. The situation was exacerbated by the fact that Merv did not want the Director of Research to get wind of his overbearing publishing habits, for the head of the department was under pressure to tighten up on expenses. The US economy was in a recession, so trading volumes were down, and TradeHouse was battling securities regulators over a scandal related to some trader nitwit's attempt to corner the US Government Bond Market. Furthermore, the offices that lined the corridor had glass walls facing the hallway, precluding any plan to hide the boxes in Merv's office. The only immediate option was to stuff as many boxes as possible into the nearby coat closet. Because it was winter, this strategy did not sit well with those looking for a place to hang their coats. Since Merv wasn't the most popular kid on the block, it didn't take long for someone, most likely the analyst with extra dry cleaning charges, to complain to the head of research. So, while the rest of the team was feverishly stuffing envelopes, down the corridor marched Don Kemp to get to the bottom of the latest Moneymax controversy. Fortunately for Merv, Kemp was simply too nice of a guy to pose a problem. He may have been a highly regarded, II-ranked analyst following the Oil Services Industry (the latest on jack-up rates, anyone?), but he was no match for someone like Merv, who didn't take no for an answer under just about any circumstance.

Over the course of the next several months, the reports were mailed out. There were even enough to send many clients a second copy. We were sure they appreciated that. With each chunk taken out of our nation's forests, a handful of people on Merv's mailing list asked to be removed so as not to receive any future mailings. The *Encyclopedia* wasn't mailed alone; Merv came up with other items—announcements of conference calls were his favorites—to slip in the envelopes, even though the clients may have already received these several times. But, as ridiculous as Merv's publishing philosophy seemed, there was a benefit (to him) of creating an unbroken paper flow. As one senior salesman noted, "The shit that Moneymax puts out works."

Sending faxes was the primary means of getting a message out to a mass audience quickly in the early 1990s. The mailroom at TradeHouse was equipped with a Sun Microsystem machine whose primary function was to do just that. This was cutting-edge technology at the time and a perfect opportunity for technology to fall into the wrong (i.e., Merv's) hands. Naturally, Merv rarely did anything himself and was incapable of operating all but the simplest of devices (public pay phones were his specialty). So he sent Jackie, his number two secretary, a nice young woman but not the sharpest knife in the drawer, to send for the umpteenth time a conference call announcement featuring, who else, but Wal-Mart. As it turned out, on the Sun Microsystem's list of published documents, the Wal-Mart Conference Call invitation was just above *The Wal-Mart Encyclopedia*. Merv asked Jackie "to Sun" the one-page conference call invitation, but she clicked on the wrong row and, you guessed it, off to hundreds of fax machines across the country was Merv's Wal-Mart tome. Well, it didn't take long for the complaints to start coming in. After all, if receiving multiple hard copies of the report weren't bad enough, now Moneymax succeeded in jamming up client's fax machines. Adding to Merv's embarrassment, most complaints, along with requests to be taken off of Merv's distribution list, were directed not to Merv, but to the institutional sales people.

Needless to say, Merv was none too pleased with Jackie, but he didn't come down hard, for Merv understood that people were not exactly lined up to come work for him and the thought of getting sidetracked from his critical role as a glorified conference planner to find a replacement was out of the question.

On the Road

Traveling with Merv, as one can imagine, was neither relaxing nor pleasant. Merv never traveled alone; he insisted that either an assistant or one of the other retail analysts accompany him. The rationale he presented to the Director of Research, who ultimately had to approve expense-related items, was that bringing two analysts to meet clients magnified the impact of the visits, and to a large extent, that was true. But the younger analysts were given limited time at the hour-long meetings, and assistants, when they were the unlucky ones, were dragged along to answer client questions that even Merv couldn't B.S. his way through, such as anything involving numbers. Perhaps even more insidiously, Merv figured there were probably people out there who didn't like him (imagine that, we thought), and if the bullets were to ever start flying, it was generally understood who would be taking one for the team and who would be seeking cover.

One person Merv failed to win over on a flight was a young stewardess who happened to spill a pot of hot coffee on him. Naturally, Merv was furious and after berating the poor young woman, demanded to be reassigned to a first-class seat. John, one of his two assistants at the time, offered the flight attendant fifty bucks to do it again, which at least brought a smile to her face.

On Wall Street, "marketing" trips connote analysts' visits to institutional client/money managers in their offices for mostly one-on-one but occasionally group meetings with the objective of maximizing II votes during the annual May surveys. To accomplish this goal, Merv preferred to concentrate his travels in the five-to-six-week period prior to the vote. While virtually all analysts at the larger Wall Street firms where the II poll was crucial also sought to accentuate their exposure during this period, most took a more realistic approach to their marketing by spreading their traveling out throughout the year.

Most analysts also use their firm's salespeople to schedule visits to clients, but not Merv. Since he was highly distrustful of anyone to do a job correctly, Merv set up his own itinerary. Many of the salespeople simply resigned themselves to the fact that this was the way it was going to be, but others voiced frustration with the intrusion and the inevitable scheduling conflicts that would arise from Merv's efforts. After he outlined the six-week campaign, which might feature the West Coast one week, the Midwest another, and the Southeast a third, and filled in the individual meetings, it was time to book flights and hotels. For these components of the marketing trip, Merv entrusted the job to his most senior secretary, Sharon. But Merv never made anything simple and easy, and since his lack of trust extended to the travel industry, most notably the airlines, he insisted on "double-booking" all of his flights. That way, surmised Merv, if a flight was canceled or if he was running late (very unlikely), he would still be able to stick with the rigid schedule. The airlines, of course, hated this, and costs ultimately landed on TradeHouse's books. On one trip to the Southeast, Merv and Bill touched down in five cities in one day, an insane schedule made virtually impossible today because of heightened security protocol. Merv also insisted on an aisle seat with his traveling companion seated in an aisle seat just across from him. That way, Merv could give his assistant plenty of work before nodding off for his nap. An aisle seat also afforded Merv the opportunity to muscle his way off of planes a bit more quickly. Never missing a chance to abuse his position to get the upper hand, Merv also insisted on boarding a plane before the bedraggled masses, even if his row was not called by the flight attendants. Rarely, if ever, did one make him wait his turn.

Often included in Merv's travels, was a marketing trip to Europe. Bill loved going "across the pond" since he really hadn't experienced Europe, and an all-expenses-paid trip made traveling with Merv worth it, or so it seemed. These trips were just as manic as an extended domestic voyage and, in some ways, even more ludicrous. The journeys often commenced with a "red-eye" flight to the United Kingdom, followed by a "hop-and-skip" jaunt across the Continent. Stops in some cities could be measured in hours and may have just involved a lunch presentation. One such trip, however, resulted in an overnight stay in Paris. "Wow", thought Bill, "how bad can this be even if I have to hang out with Merv?"

The hotel was just off of the Champs Elysees. Business travelers generally don't stay in flea-bag hotels, and Wall Street was no exception. For dinner, in the interest of time, of course, the nondescript restaurant just down the street was good enough for Merv, for tomorrow was a big day and there were memos to write. After they ate, Bill convinced Merv that a walk along Paris's most famous boulevard would help them digest their food. No sooner had they turned onto the street, Merv was ready to head back. So much for pleasantries. After returning to the hotel, Merv gave Bill some memos and report drafts to read over and asked him to bring the edited versions to Merv's room when finished. Apparently the heat was not to Merv's satisfaction, and he had called the hotel's front office to complain. So when Bill arrived at Merv's room, he was greeted by Merv in a bathrobe and shower shoes with a towel dried head (no comb-over this time) and an unhappy engineer trying to adjust the room's radiator. This episode didn't do much for the French's perception of Americans.

Whether Merv traveled domestically or overseas, when the plane landed at the end of the trip, he had one thing in mind. No, not what you think, but a visit to his chiropractor. We were never certain of the urgency of these visits—our speculation was that these daily appointments spurred his frantic departure from the office each day—for Merv did not appear to be suffering physically in any major way, but as soon as he bolted from the plane he made a beeline to the nearest pay phone to lock in a quick visit. In fact, Merv had two chiropractors that he saw on a regular basis, with one serving as a backup in case Chiropractor Number One was unavailable.

Was it possible that Merv suffered from the lingering effects of his military service? Yeah, right. Bill was too young to be called into serving his country during the Vietnam War, but Merv wasn't. At some point during his early adulthood, Merv was a member of the US Army Reserve. No one would have been surprised if he used this service as a way to finagle his way out of harm's way. Whatever the circumstances, Merv would often reference to male clients, mostly, of his days "in the Army" in an attempt to inject some testosterone into his background. As if that would impress Paul Carter, CFO of Wal-Mart.

Investment Banking—Calling the Shots and Holding the Gun

Back in the 1990s, before the dot-com bubble burst—an event that helped to uncover serious improprieties in the relationships between corporate finance and research, ultimately resulting in major regulatory changes that affected how these departments interacted with one another—research departments were largely subservient to investment bankers. The basic dynamic was corporate finance paid about half of the research department's budget, so it was only natural that research analysts helped bankers maximize their fee revenues. Bankers win underwriting and other investment banking assignments by building relationships with the CEOs and CFOs of public and private companies and by convincing these decision makers that their Wall Street firm is best suited to manage the IPO process and the period following the stock or bond offering. When a company decides to go public by offering equity, it will want the underwriter's stock analyst to cover the company and write favorable opinions. Before the wall between research and banking was strengthened, it was understood that with the exception of the most unusual circumstances, research analysts would initiate research coverage on underwriting clients with Buy or Strong Buy ratings, and managements of these companies could ask the analysts of their intentions during so-called "pitches" when the various investment banks would campaign for the lucrative underwriting assignments.

Like most businesses—although Wall Street is certainly unlike most industries in the United States—there are companies with competitive advantages that command greater market shares than their peers and weaker players with inferior business models and assets. TradeHouse Securities built its reputation and fortune on its prowess as a trading house and not as an investment bank. With the financial markets soaring and other firms and their managers getting rich taking companies public and orchestrating mergers and acquisitions during the 1980s, TradeHouse sought to become a more balanced entity by building up its banking operation. To be sure, there were more than a few qualified "rainmakers" among TradeHouse's senior bankers, but there were also plenty who were not in the upper echelon, compared with their peers at other firms.

The consumer banking team at TradeHouse fell into the latter camp. So while other firms were coining money underwriting offerings by the likes of Staples, OfficeMax, and Lowe's, TradeHouse was stuck with Rhode's Furniture and Vans. To be fair, TradeHouse had its success stories, including managing several massive bond offerings by Federated Department Stores. But in many cases, their efforts resembled "the gang that couldn't shoot straight." In one such example, Caldor Discount Stores was planning to go public, and one of the senior TradeHouse bankers who was not part of the consumer group had a strong relationship with the CEO. To position TradeHouse as a participant (hopefully, lead manager) in any upcoming offering, the banker arranged a meeting with Caldor's senior management and TradeHouse's research analyst. The purpose of this type of meeting is essentially two-fold: the analyst is given the opportunity to learn more about the company and industry, while the senior management gets to meet the analyst who will ultimately cover his company. The problem was Merv should have been representing the face of retail research given his twenty years of experience as one of the top-ranked analysts and his coverage of Wal-Mart and Kmart, two of Caldor's competitors. Merv, however, did not see the merit in spending time on this potential piece of business, and those who could compel him to participate didn't step up to the plate to ensure that TradeHouse had the greatest chance of positioning the firm for the business. So it fell to Bill to accompany the banker on the trip to the company's headquarters in Connecticut. Bill did his homework and went to the meeting prepared with a long list of questions. The meeting proceeded smoothly until the end, when the CEO asked Bill what his rating would be on his company when he publishes a report. Bill was caught off guard by what he considered an inappropriate query, even by 1990s standards. An analyst's investment rating is supposed to reflect an objective, independent opinion based on thorough research, financial projections, and a determination whether a stock's price suggests the equity is under- or over-valued. While it was generally understood that analysts would "support" companies taken public by the firms they worked for, the blatant interjection by Caldor's leader was aggressive. Senior analysts certainly understood this. Bill quickly realized he was making a rookie mistake, and after a brief hesitation blurted out, "Buy!" The CEO smiled, they all shook hands, and the banker and Bill left the building.

When they reached the sidewalk, the banker turned to face Bill and sternly noted, "When a CEO asks what your rating will be on his company, I want you to jump up and down on the table and scream, 'Buy, Buy, Buy!'" Bill apologized, got into the car with the banker for the ride back to Manhattan, and figured no harm done. Well, not exactly, for no sooner did Bill return to his office, the Director of Research called him into his office to ask what went wrong at the Caldor meeting because the banker was not pleased with his performance. Bill was tempted to question why Merv did not attend the meeting if it was so important, but wisely buttoned his lip. When a Wall Street firm is competing for investment banking business, the bankers often pull out all the stops. For large, highly visible public offerings such as the recent IPO of Facebook, it is not unusual for the CEO of the investment bank to participate in the "Pitch" to win the mandate. While Caldor certainly did not qualify as the deal of the century, underwriting fees for even a small deal could be in the millions of dollars. Consequently, it was standard procedure for a firm's most senior analyst covering that industry to attend this meeting. Even though the visit to Caldor was a preliminary "meet-and-greet", Merv's failure to attend was evidence of his selfish attitude and unwillingness to be a team player.

The attempt to win a piece of the Boise Office Products offering was an even bigger fiasco. Since the company was based in the Chicago area, pitching for this business meant a trip to the Windy City. Outside of New York, Chicago was Bill's favorite city, so the trip itself wasn't the problem. Because Bill followed the office products retailers, Boise was up his alley, and not Merv's. But there were two aspects of this assignment that increased his anxiety: first, the lead bankers for the upcoming underwriting were already chosen, and they were sizing up co-manager candidates; and second, Christine Sawtelle, the head of the consumer retail banking group had scheduled a two-week summer vacation, and she wasn't about to interrupt her holiday. The plan was to get one of the bankers from TradeHouse's Chicago office to fill in. Not only did the substitute fail to have a relationship with Boise, but he had never even met the executives. As the squirrely banker from the lead underwriter ineffectively tried to suppress his pleasure in seeing a rival firm shoot itself in the foot, Bill realized the folly in the whole expedition. He also wasn't surprised when the TradeHouse bankers pinned the blame on Bill for the failure to win the assignment.

Seamen's Furniture was another hand grenade Bill had to field. The head consumer banker wasn't as interested in the regional furniture retailer, which was already a public company, as she was interested in a Florida-based company called Rooms to Go that was founded by Morty Seaman, who was no longer running Seaman's Furniture. To help win him over, she wanted Bill to initiate research coverage of Seaman's with, naturally, a favorable report. Bill had mixed feelings about covering Seaman's since the stock had a very thin float with very low trading volume, so the clients and sales force would have very little, if any, interest. On the other hand, Bill understood the importance of being a team player and helping banking. So, after performing some basic due diligence—a couple of visits to Seaman's headquarters and stores, building financial models, and studying the furniture industry—he was ready to write a report. After Bill published his report on the company with a Buy rating on the shares, the CEO of the company complained to the head consumer banker that the report did not meet his expectations, even though for a stock that many days did not even trade, the twenty-page report seemed perfectly sufficient by most standards. Unfortunately for Bill, Merv, with whom his relationship was by now irreparably damaged, provided no line of defense when the head of consumer banking expressed her displeasure.

The End of a Working Relationship

To state that Merv was a control freak would be an egregious understatement. He trusted no one and had no problem listening in on your phone calls or prescreening your mail. The phone lines were set up so that Merv's phone would indicate when a team member was on his phone, with nothing to prevent him from eavesdropping, which he would frequently do. There was also a central mailroom on the thirty-sixth floor, with a mail slot for each person. Merv, usually on one of his numerous trips back from the bathroom, would swing by the mailroom and collect the mail for his team, paying close attention to the sender. Incoming faxes were also sorted by the mail clerks and placed in the same slots as the regular pieces of mail.

An important Connecticut-based client who liked to trade stocks around earnings announcements would poll sell-side analysts on certain stocks. They accomplished this by sending out via fax a simple spreadsheet asking the analysts for their sales, margin, and earnings estimates for certain companies. Naturally, it would be completely irresponsible not to respond as quickly as possible. It was during one of his 5:00 forays into Merv's trash for unused items that Bill found it. There, staring him in the face was the fax from Harbor Investors, snatched from his mail slot by Moneymax and tossed into the trash in an unmistakable attempt to discredit Bill in the eyes of an important account. Bill exploded. Grabbing the fax from the garbage, he stormed down to the research director's office, flashed the paper in front of him while spilling the beans.

Given the serious nature of this charge, the director felt compelled to bring this issue to higher authorities at TradeHouse. Merv wasn't fired, but he was read the riot act and told that if anything like this were to reoccur, his termination would be sealed. Well, the way Merv viewed the world, you just didn't do something like that to him. It was a body-blow that left him gasping for air. Unprecedented. Bill and George were subsequently assigned a shared assistant, providing some insulation from Merv, although cooperation on group events such as the Field Trip would continue. But Merv would no longer have Bill's back, to the extent there was even the remotest chance that he would stand up for him under adversity.

The Departure

Bill left TradeHouse in mid-1995, after three-and-a-half painful years. He knew the end was near when he saw Jerry Roos walking towards Don Kemp's office for what he assumed was an interview for his job. Merv's former senior associate at Bullhorn, Jerry had left that firm some time earlier, so there was no issue with him joining TradeHouse. That's often how things get done on Wall Street; people who can pass judgment may tell you what a great job you are doing, then stick you in the back and toss you under the bus the next day.

So Bill decided not to stick around to see if he was going to be retained or shown the door. He quickly interviewed with a couple of firms and settled for a regional company based in the Midwest that recently had opened a New York office. It was nice to feel wanted and exciting to be with a company focusing on growth. As the only retail analyst, Bill had the flexibility to cover what he wanted, and being a bigger fish in a small pond had its benefits, too. Bill thrived at the smaller firm, even after it was acquired by one of the world's largest international banks. After nearly five years, he received an offer from another regional firm that he simply couldn't refuse, and didn't.

Some of Merv's team left even before Bill departed and, eventually, the rest moved on to more pleasant (and lucrative) settings. Richard jumped ship after just fifteen months of service. On Wall Street, there is no such thing as advanced notice, either when one is resigning or asked to leave. Richard walked into Don Kemp's office on a morning when two of Merv's companies were reporting financial results. Don understood all too well the motivation, so there was no drawn-out discussion. After wishing each other well, Richard went to deliver the bombshell to his boss. The timing of Richard's exit was akin to lobbing a grenade into Merv's office. Not only did he have difficulty comprehending why someone would leave such a great opportunity, but to do this on a big earnings day showed a complete lack of respect and appreciation for all that Merv had done for Richard.

Steve, who was immediately (remember, Merv didn't ruminate over these decisions) hired to replace Richard, also left after barely a year, moving to the Midwest to become a senior analyst at a highly respected firm. Merv tried to convince Steve that working for him was the superior opportunity, an assertion that dumbfounded all of us. Steve prospered at his new firm and has been one of the top-ranked retail analysts for over ten years.

Ben took his punches better than any of us, and when he had the chance to join his old boss at a leading insurance company, it was an easy decision. He returned to his former role as a fixed-income analyst with a boss who respected him and treated him with the dignity he deserved. Ben pursued his profession while living with his wife and three sons until cancer took him from us in 2008. Ben battled this disease with courage and tenacity, while never losing his wonderful personality or sense of humor. He is greatly missed.

In 1997, TradeHouse Securities agreed to merge with a large, competitor which resulted in thousands of layoffs. Most of the former TradeHouse associates who "didn't make the cut" found new jobs on Wall Street; in the case of highly regarded senior analysts, opportunities presented themselves quickly, with many of these folks joining a firm that was anxious to build up its research staff. Merv was one of those who had to find a new home, but this proved relatively easy since he was still one of the top-ranked II analysts on The Street. Ironically, he and Steve, who returned from the Midwest, were once again at the same firm, but with drastically different circumstances. Steve was guaranteed his independence from Merv by the Director of Research.

Made in the USA
Charleston, SC
28 January 2013